Thank you to the generous team who gave their time and talents to make this book possible:

Author
Amlaku B. Eshetie

Illustrators
Rebekah Mitsein and Clark College Continuing Education watercolor students including: Marla Mattson, Katie Bradley, Lee Baughman, Joyce Saulsbury, Sharon Schware, Andrea Linn, Suzy Foster, Mikiko Flynn

Creative directors
Caroline Kurtz, Jane Kurtz, and Kenny Rasmussen

Translator
Amlaku B. Eshetie

Designer
Beth Crow

Ready Set Go Books, an Open Hearts Big Dreams Project

Special thanks to Ethiopia Reads donors and staff for believing in this project and helping get it started-- and for arranging printing, distribution, and training in Ethiopia.

Trees Are Life

ዛፎች ሕይወት ናቸው

English and Amharic

Long ago, people moved
from place to place.

በጥንት ጊዜ ሰዎች ከቦታ ቦታ
ይዘዋወሩ ነበር፡፡

Trees helped them stay alive.

ዛፎች በሕይወት እንዲቆዩ የሚረዷቸው ነበሩ።

Trees were full of
things to eat.

ዛፎች የሚበሉ ነገሮችን
ይሰጧቸው ነበር።

Trees helped bring clouds and rain.

ዛፎች ዳመናዎች እንዲፈጠሩ እና
ዝናብ እንዲያገኙ ይረዱ ቸው ነበር።

Trees gave protection and shelter.

ዛፎች መከለያዎቻቸው እና መጠለያዎቻቸው ነበሩ።

Forests were huge and covered much of the earth.

ደኖች ጥቅጥቅ ያሉ እና የምድርን አብዛኛውን ክፍል የሸፈኑ ነበሩ።

Then people
began to grow
food to eat.

ከጊዜ በኋላ ግን
ሰዎች የምግብ
ሰብሎችን
ማዝመር ጀመሩ።

They began to cut trees to plant seeds.

ሰብሎቻቸውን ለሚያዘምሩበት
ቦታም ዛፎችን መመንጠር ጀመሩ።

They stopped moving
from place to place.

ከቦታ ቦታ
መዘዋወራቸውንም
አቆሙ።

More and more people were born.

ሰዎች በብዛት ተዋለዱ፤ ተባዙም።

As the years went by,
people used the wood from
more and more trees.

ብዙ ዓመታትም ተቆጠሩ፤
ሰዎችም ዛፎችን እየቆረጡ
እንጨቶችን ለተለያዩ ነገሮች
በብዛት መጠቀማቸውን ቀጠሉ።

K. Bradley

They ripped the forest cover off of the land.

ደኖቻን
ጨፍጭፈው
ምድርን
አራቆቱት።

Now many places in
Ethiopia are dry and hot.

አሁን ኢትዮጵያ ውስጥ ብዙ
ቦታዎች ደረቅና ሞቃት ናቸው፡፡

In rainy season, floods sweep away the soil.

በክረምት ጊዜም የምድሩ አፈር
በቀላሉ ይታጠባል።

People remember how trees helped them.

ሰዎች ዛፎች እንዴት ይጠቅሟቸው እንደነበር አስታወሱ።

Ethiopia wants to have many trees again.

እናም ኢትዮጵያ እንደገና ብዙ ዛፎች እንዲኖራት ፈለገች።

Ethiopian leaders came up with a plan to plant four billion trees during one rainy season.

የኢትዮጵያ መሪዎች በአንድ የክረምት ወቅት ብቻ አራት ቢሊዮን ችግኞችን ለመትከል እቅድን አቀረቡ።

Ethiopians set a
world record for tree
planting in one day.

ኢትዮጵያዊያን በአንድ
ቀን ብዙ ቁጥር ችግኞችን
የመትከል የዓለም ክብረ
ወሰንን አስመዘገቡ።

People are learning to love trees again.

ሰዎች ዛፎችን
መውደድን እንደገና
እያወቁ ነው።

Trees will help Ethiopia and the whole world stay alive.

ዛፎች ኢትዮጵያ እና መላው ዓለም
በሕይወት እንዲቆይ ይጠቅማሉ።

About the Story

According to Farm Africa, an organization working on reforestation efforts in East Africa, less than 4% of Ethiopia's land is forested, compared to around 30% at the end of the 19th century, a situation that has led to soil erosion, droughts, and flooding during the times of heavy rains. As part of its pledge to help reverse global trends, Ethiopia says that the country planted more than 353 million trees in 12 hours in July, 2019, part of a campaign dubbed "Green Legacy," widely reported to be a world record. Officials handed out seedlings for a few days before-- mostly indigenous species and also fruit trees. Communities were encouraged to protect the seedlings and continue the planting all through rainy season, usually the months of May and October. The United Nations praised the effort and called on other African countries to have their own tree planting days in hopes of helping tackle climate change.

About The Author

Amlaku's first children's book was a literacy book about the English Alphabet, Numbers, Colors, and Shapes printed in Addis Ababa, Ethiopia in 2011. This is his second children's book. He writes, "I generally love kids and wish to be contributing to their all-rounded growth somehow. As a translator to Ready Set Go Books for nearly two years, I was motivated by the ways the author of many of the books I translate, Jane Kurtz, creates and develops stories for children. She presents folktales or wise sayings in narrative and sequential ways tuned and simplified to the children's ages and levels."

He says that he tried to create a true story about teff to teach both kids of the diaspora and Ethiopia and worked on it "with a great deal of consultation and support from the experienced author, Jane, and her sister Caroline Kurtz." He adds, "I am hopeful that this inspiration will continue...Thank you Jane and Caroline! Beth Crow, thank you too for pulling together the wonderful illustrations!"

About The Illustrators

Some of the illustrations for this book came into being as a group effort by the art instructors and their students of Clark College ECD (Economic and Community Development). Katie Bradley and Lee Baughman introduced the Ready Set Go books to several of Lee's classes, and as the excitement caught on, other instructors and their classes got involved as well. Students range from beginning painters to experienced artists.

These talented artists include:
Rebekah Mitsein
Marla Mattson
Joyce Saulsbury
Sharon Schware
Andrea Linn
Suzy Foster
Mikiko Flynn
Katie Bradley
Lee Baughman

One of the watercolor painters, Mikiko Flynn, was born and raised in Japan surrounded by nature. She started painting seriously after she retired from Ophthalmology and is excited to be part of Ready Set Go Books. She writes, "My first memory of Ethiopia is when Abebe Bikila won the 1964 Tokyo Summer Olympics running the marathon, defending his gold title of previous 1960 Rome Olympics where he ran barefoot. (He wore shoes for Tokyo.) I remember all of Japan was excited about Abebe's victory.

I believe in the value of education. If it weren't for my late husband who encouraged me to study (I had finished through high education only in Japan) and pursue the dream of becoming a physician I would have never made it, especially with two small children."

About Ready Set Go Books

Reading has the power to change lives, but many children and adults in Ethiopia cannot read. One reason is that Ethiopia doesn't have enough books in local languages to give people a chance to practice reading. Ready Set Go books wants to close that gap and open a world of ideas and possibilities for kids and their communities.

When you buy a Ready Set Go book, you provide critical funding to create and distribute more books.

Learn more at:
http://openheartsbigdreams.org/book-project/

About Ethiopia Reads

Ethiopia Reads was started by volunteers in places like Grand Forks, North Dakota; Denver, Colorado; San Francisco, California; and Washington D.C. who wanted to give the gift of reading to more kids in Ethiopia.

One of the founders, Jane Kurtz, learned to read in Ethiopia where she spent most of her childhood and where the circle of life has come around to bring her Ethiopian-American grandchildren. As a children's book author, Jane is the driving force behind Open Hearts Big Dreams Ready Set Go Books - working to create the books that inspire those just learning to read.

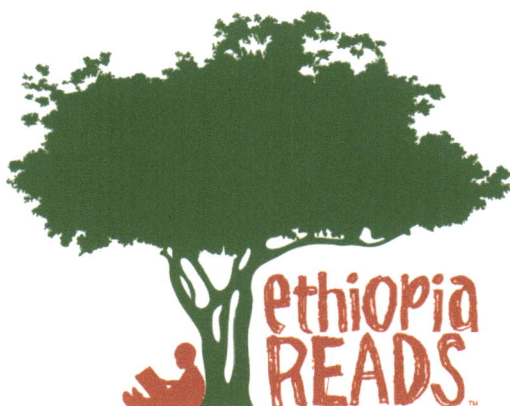

About Open Hearts Big Dreams

Open Hearts Big Dreams began as a volunteer organization, led by Ellenore Angelidis in Seattle, Washington, to provide sustainable funding and strategic support to Ethiopia Reads, collaborating with Jane Kurtz. OHBD has now grown to be its own nonprofit organization supporting literacy, innovation, and leadership for young people in Ethiopia.

Ellenore Angelidis comes from a family of teachers who believe education is a human right, and opportunity should not depend on your birthplace. And as the adoptive mother of a little girl who was born in Ethiopia and learned to read in the U.S., as well as an aspiring author, she finds the chance to positively impact literacy hugely compelling!

OPEN**HEARTS**
BIGDREAMS

About the Language

Amharic is a Semetic language -- in fact, the world's second-most widely spoken Semetic language, after Arabic. Starting in the 12th century, it became the Ethiopian language that was used in official transactions and schools and became widely spoken all over Ethiopia.

It's written with its own characters, over 260 of them. Eritrea and Ethiopia share this alphabet, and they are the only countries in Africa to develop a writing system centuries ago that is still in use today!

About the Translation

Translation is currently being coordinated by a volunteer, Amlaku Bikss Eshetie who has a BA degree in Foreign Languages & Literature, an MA in Teaching English as a Foreign Language, and PhD courses in Applied Linguistics and Communication, all at Addis Ababa University. He taught English from elementary through university levels and is currently a passionate and experienced English-Amharic translator. As a father of three, he also has a special interest in child literacy and development. He can be reached at: khaabba_ils@protonmail.com

 Chaos

 Not Ready!

 We Can Stop the Lion

 Talk Talk Turtle

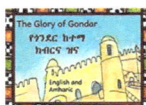 The Glory of Gondar

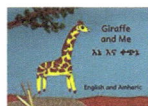 Giraffe and Me

 Fifty Lemons

 Big, Bigger, Biggest

 To view all available titles, search "Ready Set Go Ethiopia" or scan QR code

CPSIA information can be obtained
at www.ICGtesting.com
Printed in the USA
BVHW021838030622
638869BV00001B/1